HOPE
FOR FAITH

C.F. Beyers Naudé
Dorothee Sölle

HOPE FOR FAITH

a conversation

WCC Publications, Geneva
Wm. B. Eerdmans, Grand Rapids

Published by WCC Publications, Geneva, in their Risk book series, in collaboration with Wm. B. Eerdmans Publishing Co., 255 Jefferson Ave., S.E., Grand Rapids, Michigan 49503, USA.

ISBN 2-8254-0860-3 (WCC)
ISBN 0-8028-0191-9 (Eerdmans)

Original title: Hoop voor geloof

© 1985 Uitgeverij Ten Have b.v., Baarn, The Netherlands

© 1986 English edition worldwide, World Council of Churches, 150 route de Ferney, 1211 Geneva 20, Switzerland

© Photographs: NOS, Afdeling Foto, Hilversum, Netherlands

No. 31 in the Risk book series (a Risk special)

Printed in Switzerland

They are both committed Christians, active in the struggles of our day for peace and justice. They have taken a stand, in controversial areas of the life of the church and of society, and they have suffered for it.

They had never met, but they had followed each other's career from a distance. They met in the Netherlands, for the first time, on 20 June 1985. They were interviewed for IKON Television, the Dutch ecumenical broadcasting company, by Prof. Dr Lammert Leertouwer.

One of them, Rev. Dr Christiaan Frederik Beyers Naudé, is the general secretary of the South African Council of Churches. He has identified himself with the aspirations of the black people in his country, and has suffered alienation and rejection. A banning order for seven years had meant a severe curtailment of his freedom of movement.

The other, Prof. Dr Dorothee Sölle, is a German theologian, now teaching at Union Theological Seminary in New York. Reacting to the Nazi phase of her national history and to her own background of affluence, she has involved herself in the peace movement and the cause of the poor of the world.

Reproduced here is the text, unedited for the most part, of their 90-minute conversation. In it we hear the stories of their conversion to Christ and of their involvement in the struggles of our time. We hear them talking about concerns which have increasingly claimed a place on the agenda of the ecumenical movement.

A dialogue of commitments which touches on some of the most talked-about issues of our day.

HOPE
FOR FAITH

Interviewer
Two very different people: Professor Dorothee Sölle, now
teaching theology at Union Theological Seminary in New
York, and Dr Beyers Naudé, general secretary of the
South African Council of Churches. They have,
however, something in common. For many people all
over the world their very existence is a sign of hope, but
for others, among them old friends and relatives, they are
dangerous people, misguided in their hopes, confused in
their way of life, even traitors to the best traditions of the
Christian church: heretics, to say the least.

Dr Sölle, how well do you know this Rev. Beyers Naudé,
and what makes it so important for you to meet him?

Sölle
I believe the significance of our meeting has to do
with our Christian heritage and its future. Beyers,
reading through some of what you did and lived through
in the last years, I have wondered about your inner
growth and development — but these are just ordinary
words. What I really mean is much more spiritual. It
is called conversion, it's turning round from one way
to another one, and that is, I think, what interests me
most about your life and the life of all my fellow
Christians, and my own life as well: How does God
work with us in our times and convert us from our
wrong ways?

Interviewer
So let that be the first theme of this discussion. I
would like to show you a picture, Dr Sölle. Do you
recognize this typical Afrikaaner dominee* to the left,
member of the Broederbond, firmly rooted in South
African society? And are you able to understand that it
is the same man you are talking to?

---

* Pastor

Sölle
Not easily!

Interviewer
Dr Naudé, what happened to the man in this photo?

Beyers Naudé
Well, I wouldn't blame Dorothee if she said: "I don't recognize the man and I don't recognize at all or understand what has happened to you." I perhaps should say that I come from a very conservative, deeply religious Afrikaaner home. My father was also a minister of religion, steeped in the Calvinist tradition, strong, very strong in his feelings of loyalty to his people, a patriot in the best sense of the word, as seen by the Afrikaaner people. He fought in the Anglo-Boer war, on the side of the Boers, had a deep friendship with one of the generals called Christaan Frederick Beyers — that is why my name is not a family name. I was named after General Beyers, who died shortly before I was born. So in that sense my whole background is one of a deeply religious, strongly nationalist Afrikaaner tradition.

I know that many people find it difficult to understand how it has been possible for somebody coming from that background, with my whole education, my position which I held in the Dutch Reformed Church (the NG Kerk), where I was elected moderator of one of the regional synods, with the fact that for 23 years I was a member of the secret Afrikaans organization called the Afrikaaner Broederbond — for somebody like that to become what I have become today. What happened to me?

I think there are three major factors which contributed to my conversion. The first is a theological one. When, after the Second World War, in looking at what was happening in Africa, the whole process of decolonization, freedom — political freedom — coming to Africa, the cry of millions of Africans throughout the continent to throw off the yoke of colonialism, with my deep interest in mission, in evangelism, and in the youth work of the church, I asked myself: "What does this say to us in South Africa?"

Of course I knew the stand which my church had taken with regard to apartheid. And that led me to a self-study of the traditional ways in which the Dutch Reformed Church justified the whole policy of apartheid on biblical grounds. I did this study in between, and eventually came to the conclusion that there was no way in which I could justify on biblical grounds the whole policy of apartheid, as was done by my church. There was no way I could subscribe to the interpretation which they gave to certain passages of the Old and the New Testament. These were either unconsciously or deliberately so distorted, so one-sided, so politically or ideologically motivated and loaded, that for the first time, you know, there was this theological crisis in my life.

But I was afraid to make this known because I knew, with my position of leadership in the church, with my position in the Broederbond, that if I started to express these new convictions in public, it would lead to a tremendous storm, reaction, protest, anger and rejection.

Sölle
May I interrupt you and ask a question out of my own tradition? I am a German, living after Auschwitz, and when you just said how the tradition of your church has justified and legitimized apartheid theology, I recalled that in my country, the "Deutsche Christen"

justified National Socialism and tried to ground their racism and their Führer principle on some misinterpreted Christian tradition. Would that be a parallel for you?

Beyers Naudé
No doubt about it. At that stage of my study, I didn't know that. But in the course of my study I came to the shocking conclusion that there were many parallels, painful parallels, frightening parallels, between what had happened in the period of Nazi Germany, especially within the church, and what we were trying to do to justify a racist and unjust policy. At first I was unwilling to admit that — it was painful, too painful — but eventually I was forced to do so. I am not saying they are identical, but there are very strong parallels, and that led me to the discovery eventually that I could not any longer support it. But I kept it to myself. I was very afraid to express it in public.

And then I think of a second event in my life, or a series of events, which subsequently I saw to be, if I may describe it in this way, the hand of God guiding me into a new direction. It was the fact that I was elected as acting moderator of the Transvaal Synod, and in that position, young ministers — white ministers — who were serving African and coloured and Indian congregations came to me with the problems which they were experiencing within their own congregations, the painful experiences of their own people with what apartheid laws were doing to them. And when they came to me and described what they themselves had experienced, I could not believe it. I knew them well, because they were students when I was a university pastor in Victoria. There was a very fine, open, warm relationship between us and I said to them: "It's impossible, it can't be." And then they invited me to go to their congregations, which I did. I met with their church councils, I met with members of the congregation, I met with families who were deeply divided because, for instance, of the mixed marriages act, and the group areas act, and I was shattered. It was an experience which led me to the situation of being totally lost.

And then came Sharpeville — that was the third event. On 21 March 1960, a peaceful protest march of people was disrupted by 69 people being shot, most of them in their back when they fled, and that in a certain sense culminated the whole situation. And there was no way in which I could get out of it any longer.

Sölle
And then to think that this spring they did it again!

Beyers Naudé
Subsequently I recognized it as the way in which God in a certain sense had guided me all along and said to me, "OK, I'll give you the time to think about it, to reflect upon it", but all of a sudden there was that crisis and there was no option, except to stand by what I then had discovered to be the truth.

Interviewer
You were speaking about crisis and fear, so can we ask you, Dr Sölle, what happened to that upper middle-class liberal German girl who has now become Dorothee Sölle? You must know fear and you must have known very deep dangers in your life.

Sölle
I think one root of my changing, and continuing to change, has to do with my national identity, being a German, and not denying that at any point, inheriting

this terrible heritage which I cannot wash off me. It's just a part of my life to be a German, to think in that language, to talk, and to know what was done to the Jewish people in the name of my country, "im Namen des Deutschen Volkes". I cannot help thinking of the people who were killed in the gas chambers and concentration camps. To think of them is a lifelong learning process, a kind of quest for truth. Why did that happen? Why did those nice people who played the violoncello and read Goethe do all these things, or at least tolerate them? What happened to them? What were the deepest reasons? It's not just one demon called Adolf Hitler — that's ridiculous. I ask not only my country but also my class — the bourgeois class: How come that this class so often pretended not to know, not to have anything to do with it? How is this related to our present stage?

And I would like to make a remark about apartheid, what that means to me. Three or four years ago I met two young white students from your country, Beyers, in the United States. We got to talk a little bit and I asked them about the situation in South Africa, and about the situation of black people, and specifically about whether they knew Soweto, whether they had been there, whether they knew if the people had water or not in their huts or barracks, if they had electricity or oil or not — very specific questions. And they didn't know a thing. They knew the golf and tennis places where they used to play. They knew their little schools, they knew how beautiful their country was. They gave me a story as if they were talking for a travel agent. They told me how beautiful that country is, and they did not respond to any of my more and more specific questions because they didn't know. They simply did not know the reality of their own country. There is an invisible wall which is much worse than the Berlin wall in my country, a wall that is most terrible.

I think most of the people of my country live behind that wall because apartheid is not just a South African problem. It's a problem of the rich world and the so-called first world that we live in apartheid, that we live behind that wall and we know about the nice cheap bananas and nice coffee we get from these poor countries and we know of a lot of things we can have and buy, and go to, but our perspective is still the perspective of a tourist and not the perspective of a sister or a brother.

Beyers Naudé
May I respond and make some remarks on that? You remind me of one of the most painful aspects of our life in South Africa; we do not know.

I constantly ask myself, how is it possible that a community, in this case a white community, deeply religious, claiming to be devoutly Christian, building its whole life — or claiming to build its life, and also its political structure — on the recognition of God's sovereignty as it is stated in our constitution; how is it possible that we could, for instance, remove forcibly three and a half million people from their land, from where they live, from where they had settled down, from where they are happy as a community, force them into arid, remote areas where the possibility of livelihood, of income, of existence is in fact so small that for all practical purposes it is a process of slow death which they are facing?

Sölle
It indeed is, and how do we answer that question?

Beyers Naudé
And, you know, I must feel the agony of this, especially because I know that the people who are in control and in power doing this, these are my people. I cannot deny

that I am an Afrikaaner. I don't want to deny it. How can I? I am nothing else but an Afrikaaner, and yet in that sense I don't see myself to be there — then the agony of that separation. What are the basic roots, what are the deepest roots of such an injustice, of such inhumanity? How do we continue to justify it, and that in the face of the fact that the whole world outside is turning like South Africa. This is wrong, this is inhuman, and this is evil. I am still struggling because I find certain answers but yet I sense here in myself this is not yet the full answer. There is some deeper perspective of human existence, of human justification of such acts which I have not yet been able to discover.

Sölle
Yes, I do believe that it is a theological problem, and not just political or social, as they always tell us.

Interviewer
Do you agree?

Beyers Naudé
I fully agree.

Sölle
It is a question of faith and not just a question of reason. It is our faith which is touched on in those questions. And I have this question — that's another thing I would like to ask you; when you were converted to fight apartheid and to go along with your black brothers and sisters and develop at the same time a sort of liberation theology which comes out of the struggle, why did other people in your church not go along with you, or why did they stay where they were, almost immobile, immovable?

This is also my question about my church, and my
country, at the time of this great awakening, as I would
like to call the peace movement since 1979 in my country,
when millions and millions of people went on the street and
wanted to fight that general apartheid we have in the
world between the rich and the poor. Why do we need so
many bombs and weapons of death, they asked. They
understood quite well why they went on the streets. But
there was a split in the church as well, and many young
people went out on the streets, and many young pastors
went, and many church synods and groups and hierarchies
stayed aside or stayed in a wishy-washy, what we call a "ja-
nein" position, saying "ja" and "nein" at the same time!
But why is that so, why couldn't we reach them, why
couldn't we move together, as one group? It's one of my
deepest wishes to see that coming true in my life-time.

Beyers Naudé
I think the first reason, from my side, is that in the
Afrikaaner society there is such a deep sense of loyalty to
a wrong concept. Loyalty to your people, loyalty to
your country, loyalty and patriotism, have in a certain
sense become deeply religious values; they have been
converted into deeply religious values. So that
anybody who is seen to be disloyal to his nation, to his
people, is not only deemed to be a traitor, but in the
deeper sense of the word, he is seen as betraying God.
He is betraying the deepest values of the understanding
of faith as it was portrayed. So again the basic problem
is not an economic one or a cultural one or a social one,
although all these factors play a role, in the deep sense
of unity of the Afrikaaner people.

The fact is that you are allowed to have your
differences among your Afrikaaner people, but only to
a degree. You must know where the boundary is, the
limits of dissent and of disagreement. The moment you

12

overstep that boundary — and that line is very finely
drawn and invisible — the moment you overstep it
you are totally out. You are ostracized, you are pushed
aside, you are seen to be a traitor and, humanly
speaking, you are never taken back. And I think in my
case it was due to the fact that the Afrikaaner people
see themselves to be a minority, feel themselves to
be threatened, and their whole history has been built
up on the basis of fear. There was the threat, you
know, from the black majority, the threat from British
imperialism, the threat coming from others. Hence their
mentality of the besieged, that "lager" mentality, in
which our people always felt that true patriotism and
true loyalty meant you stand by your people regardless
of questions of right and wrong.

Sölle
I couldn't agree more, in regard to my own country.
There is a deeply grounded wrong understanding of
God's intention with us, in the understanding of
salvation as salvation of individuals who will be freed
from this more or less bad world which never can be
changed. It's not an understanding of the kingdom of
God, it's about the salvation of the ego in a way, so
individualism is really at the heart of this form of
religion. I think there are some differences in terms of
nationalism because in Western Europe, or at least in
Germany, I do believe that nationalism died in 1945,
more or less, when instead of that we got a new
identity which was made up of belonging to the West,
economically first of all, militarily, and politically in
our political system. As soon as we move away from
the Western culture and the Western ideals we are
blamed; we are no good as Germans, no good as
democrats or whatever. The most natural accusation
they level against those who disagree or register dissent
is, of course, as it is in your case, that we are all
communists, paid by Moscow, as everyone knows!
Whenever you disagree with this golden calf, and
say: "No, that is not the God who led us out of
Egypt, this is not our God", then they tell you you are
a commie.

Beyers Naudé
That's right.

Sölle
You get this all the time, in soft or less soft forms.

Interviewer
Have you been ostracized as Dr Beyers Naudé said that
he was?

Sölle
Yes, I could say so. I mean, I am not teaching in my own country, but in a more, theologically speaking, liberal country, which the United States in many ways still is.

Interviewer
You would like to be a professor of theology in Germany now?

Sölle
Years ago I had this idea, this intention, but it just didn't work out for several reasons. One was surely my being a woman. Then there were the political and theological questions. I'm not bitter about that; it's simply a fact of life. I think my theological development made a big step forward when I learned

things from my brothers and sisters in the third world. What I had looked for or tried to grasp was a sort of political theology, but they gave me this beautiful new term and concept, theology of liberation, and since then I have tried to do a theology of liberation for first world citizens in my own country. That means, of course, that you get ostracized; you get into trouble with family and friends, and many other people, and the media, etc., etc. They just make you into a non-person.

Beyers Naudé
That's right.

Interviewer
Do you recognize that?

Beyers Naudé
Yes, I do. And the moment they succeed in making you a non-person, whatever you say, therefore, loses significance and loses meaning, and therefore in that sense they invalidate what you are saying, and thereby, as it were, remove the danger that the ideas and the thoughts that you present could therefore have some impact. I think that was one intention of the banning order put on me, for seven years, you know. The Germans have got a beautiful word, a vivid description which says: they make you "mundtot". No word, no sign, no life. That's the only way in which they can deal with it.

But what really puzzles me, and perhaps you could help me here, is that you have got the freedom of speech, for instance in the German community, in society and the church. Look at all your publications, look at all your newspapers, your media — everybody is free to express his or her opinion. And I sense this, for instance when I think of the Kirchentag. I saw there thousands of young people coming together, sincerely seeking after truth, meaningful life, the relationship of their Christian faith to their living and to the problems all over the world. I mean, in the mornings, you know, I saw six to seven thousand young people sitting there, in eight of the different halls, doing Bible study, and yet at the same time I hear the complaint all around Germany that the young people are no longer in the church. Well then, to me the question immediately arises: not what is wrong with the young people but what is wrong with the church?

Sölle
Sure, and as soon as the church wakes up from this apartheid theology, as I would call it — it's almost like in scholasticism when the theologians debated how many angels could stand on a needle's point. So is in a way dealing with theology in terms of the sixteenth century, removing theology from reality, from our problems today. How should we, where do we invest our money, for example? Do we invest it with Dresdnerbank which makes its profit from South African business life? Do we go ahead and buy South African Outspan oranges, or do we protest that and tell our people this tastes like blood?

These are the questions we try to bring into the church bodies. These are the things we discuss with people; we tell them that this is the way Christ is crucified today, and that you can't develop any piety outside all of this and independent of all of this, keeping yourself clean from reality. I do believe that there is a deep religious need, or a desire to learn more about religion, to hear, to understand what it is all about. There is a deep thirst. But this cannot be the answer, you can't give them coca-cola for that. And there is a sort of a churchy coca-cola around, and people are really beginning to understand that this doesn't help them.

Beyers Naudé
But the young people, they are too shrewd, they've
got that inner sensitivity, they've got that basic honesty,
in fact that brutal honesty, in which they will listen and
they will consider, they will reflect, and they will
eventually come to the conclusion that in no way what
this person is saying reflects reality as I see it, what I
believe to be the truth as I experience it. And that is
my basic problem also with regard to what is
happening in our country.

Interviewer
How about young people in your country?

Beyers Naudé
Well, could I just try to answer by saying that
whenever anybody asks me a question about my
country, I've always got to reply with a question first.
Which part of the people are we talking about? The
white sector or the black sector? Because the division is
so deep that for all practical purposes the responses,
the values, the valuation also, you know, are always
basically different. As far as the young white people
are concerned, the majority of the young white
people in South Africa live to a large degree in
ignorance of what is happening, or even if they are
aware they are not concerned, they are not involved, it
doesn't affect them so deeply, and even when it does,
some of them are afraid that it does.

Interviewer
So they cannot be the young people you put so much
of your hopes in?

Beyers Naudé
No, certainly not. If I have to put my hope in South
Africa on the youth, it is first of all the black youth,

who are responding, who are sacrificing their lives, who are trying to give a message to South Africa and to the world in a way which is, to many, shocking, totally unacceptable, painful. They are saying: "Sorry, we don't understand your Christian life and Christian faith as you portray it. To us it has no relevance, no meaning. We want to see a concrete, living example of justice, of righteousness, of love, of truth, of liberation." The moment they see something of that in a minister or a priest, or a person who calls himself or herself a Christian, there is a response.

Now, if that's the case, then I ask myself, why is it that we also in South Africa, as the church, don't hear this, why is it that we are not more sensitive to it? And respond to it, instead of waiting until a situation of such conflict arises, where young people are forced to take up stones and to throw them, to make Molotov cocktails and to use them, and then to be condemned by a large sector of the Christian community, inside and outside the country, for doing what they are doing? Why do we do it, instead of asking ourselves, are we not the ones who are basically to be blamed, that we allowed a situation to develop where these young people were forced into such an action on their part?

Sölle
It comes to my mind that Gandhi, who was the apostle of non-violence, was once asked whether he would fight Hitler with non-violence as well, and he said "no", he could not, because against Hitler he had to use violence. And this was said by the hero of non-violence, and I think the ANC in a way says the same thing. They tried so hard — it's a terrible story, the history of the African fight for freedom in your country, how long they went along with non-violence

and how bloodily they were beaten down, just as the
people of Gandhi were beaten down again and again,
the harmless people who did nothing — like Sharpeville,
and the worst thing about Sharpeville is that it continues.
Just this year we had it again, the same story, as if
nothing had happened.

Beyers Naudé
And it was on the very day, you know this is what
makes it so terrible, on the very day, 25 years later, of
the commemoration of Sharpeville: twenty people,
marching peacefully to a funeral, are shot and killed.
Then the question arises, do we never learn? And
what is the response on the part of the Christian
community?

Talking about the ANC, normally it is not known
that the ANC was established in 1912, two years after
the Union of South Africa was established; it was
organized in protest against the establishment of the
Union of South Africa, where the legitimate rights of the
black community were deeply affected and, in fact,
rejected. For 48 years the African National Congress
stood as a totally peaceful political organization,
trying to build the resistance on peaceful lines —
Luthuli, you know, the well-known leader of the ANC,
winner of the Nobel Prize, an advocate of non-violence
up till the day of his death. And you know, what affected
my life very deeply was this. For the first time I began to
read the history of the ANC and, to my shame I must
say, I had no knowledge even of the existence of the
ANC up till 1960. It is terrible, but it is true!

And when for the first time I began to read this, my
first question was, during these 48 years was there any
church in South Africa which officially supported those
goals and the striving for justice and for liberation on the
part of the majority of the people? As far as I know there

was not a single resolution which was adopted by any
church, or by any synod during those 48 years in favour
of expressing themselves in moral support of that striving
for justice. Individuals, yes, but not the church as a
whole, and again that brought up for me the painful
question, what is wrong in our own understanding and
proclamation of the faith that we live in that kind of a
cocoon which we spin around ourselves, happily
warm, ensconced in it, and the world outside — don't
worry, that's their problem!

Interviewer
Both of you seem to be very disappointed in the
church, in your own church, in the church as such. Is
there any future for this church?

Sölle
You know, I do believe we live in a time where this
marriage between the church and the capitalist order is
breaking. The divorce is not yet through, but it will
come. Time works for the divorce of church and
capitalism, and we have to work inside of this process
and free the church from the stranglehold of believing
in the values of capitalism, and not seeing God's work
beyond that system. And I am not absolutely hopeless.
I am sceptical about my own church in West Germany
because of its very special structure as a Volkskirche,
with all that money behind it. I think perhaps my church
will come last; after all other churches are converted to
Jesus Christ, then finally even the West German
Church will be converted to Christ. When I look
around, look to the East, to East Germany, and what
they say in the church about peace, and to Holland, our
two neighbours, they are far ahead of ours, my church.
What our churches say is weak, unclear, shaky, gives no
clear direction to the people. They are not able to

condemn what has to be condemned today. They are
not able to say it is a sin to build nuclear weapons,
not to speak of using them, etc. etc. In all of this, I am
not so sceptical about God's work elsewhere, but I
think it starts again as it did in the New Testament,
with the poor, and not with the rich.

Beyers Naudé
If I could respond to that, I think it depends on what we
mean by the church. If we mean by the church mainly
the institution, the structure, the visible, traditional
symbols, then I believe that the church, in that sense,
will experience one crisis after another, until it
comes to the recognition, understanding, that the
church, in the real sense of the word, is where the
people of God are, where life is being discovered again,
the true meaning of love, of human community, of
mutual concern for one another, of caring of people,
of seeking true meaningful relationship, understanding
between people, not only between Christians but
between all people. Therefore, in that sense I am
very hopeful about what is happening, not only in our
country, but also in other countries, because there are
new perspectives, of the Christian faith and of truth,
which are being discovered and which are being, as it
were, agonized about by so many small groups of
people. Tremendously encouraging insights and
examples are coming through. If I think of South
Africa, what encourages me is the fact that
sometimes the most meaningful revelation about a new
understanding of the Christian faith and about the
Christian church and about Christian community comes
from the poorest, comes from those communities which
are normally not seen to be the ones with authority or
with power, or comes from those who normally never
believe themselves to have any real message. But

when you begin to listen to what they are saying, it is
absolutely marvellous, and then to discover how little
I know and how much I need to be constantly
converted, in my whole understanding, in my whole
willingness, therefore, in true humility to sit at the feet
of such people, and learn and hear. And in that sense
I believe there is a tremendous future for the
Christian community in the world.

Sölle
I agree...

Interviewer
Only if it converts itself to the true gospel?

Sölle
Yes, but who is the church? I think the growth of the
true church today comes not from within but from the
outside, from the peace groups, from the women's
groups, from those groups who in certain fields of post-
Christian culture live and think and understand more
and more the meaning of the gospel, rather than those
who claim to be the masters of the gospel, namely
those white male, middle-class theologians. These
groups appropriate the gospel precisely the way you
described it, in sharing in understanding our lives
together in the light of the gospel. I don't put my hope
so much on the youth as such, I think that's a sort of a
myth, but I do put my hope much more on women, on
women's groups inside the first world. Women who
are so frustrated with that culture in which we live,
that apartheid, this cultural apartheid, the brutality,
the competitiveness, and all those factors of our life,
that they have to distance themselves from — just to
stay human or become human.

I think that there is a growth of faith in new forms
all over the world, and some of the signs of it are very
classical signs, it's base communities — and you may
speak to that more than I can — it is martyrdom, which
is one of the classical signs of where does the church
live and grow. We in the first world, in relative
freedom, don't experience martyrdom in the strict
sense of the word. But I think we have to prepare
ourselves and others in our midst for more restrictions,
discrimination. The price to be a Christian will be
higher in the next twenty years, will become higher and
higher; it will be much tougher, if you really want to be
a Christian.

Interviewer
And will the rewards also be higher, do you think?
In Holland we have a commercial attitude. We want to
know what we invest in!

Sölle
Yes, I think Christ didn't promise us victory. I think
that would be an illusion. Christ promised us life, and
that includes death. Christ didn't tell us that we
would win. Other people tell us that all the time, but
I think it would be too superficial to think that way.
We hope to win; we fight to win; we give our blood
and our lives to win and free ourselves in others, but I
think we cannot understand our own struggle in terms
of success and non-success.

Interviewer
You are seventy years old now, Dr Naudé, you
should know.

Beyers Naudé
Could I perhaps add to that by saying that one of the
most wonderful discoveries which I have made in this

pilgrimage of my life is that there comes a moment when you don't look for a reward any longer, you don't feel it is important at all. What is of importance to you is your experience of life, of an inner peace, of a strength of faith, of a continuation of your commitment, however weak it may be, and of the fact that you simply forget, you simply do not regard the traditional value systems which have been built up in you and around you to be meaningful any longer. Money? Well, you certainly need money to live, but money, in the sense of the word that it becomes a symbol therefore of security and value? Popularity, world acclaim? That was perhaps one of the most meaningful experiences of my life in this pilgrimage which I go through. Take, for instance, the fact that so many of the traditional values which were portrayed to me unconsciously — I don't think it was done deliberately by my father or my mother because they were deeply devout people, and I respect them for the fact that they gave us the very best according to their understanding. But I had to discover that so many of these values simply lost their meaning for me, and therefore an inner peace of mind came, also a loss of fear, that even if somebody asked me I'd say, well, suppose you go back, suppose now that you are being threatened, suppose that you may lose your life tomorrow, then, well, my response is, well if that happens, so what? Isn't then the death which you experience as a result of what you try to be in the deepest sense of the word, isn't that then something in a certain sense of a crowning of your whole life and what you try to convey?

People many times ask me, but don't you get tired? You know you have been fighting now for how many years? Since 1960, it's now 25 years. My wife many times has asked me, Beyers, constantly you are repeating the same concern, you are stating the same conviction. Don't you get tired? And then my response is, yes certainly, at times I get tired, physically tired, but if you ask me whether in my mind or in my being, in my inmost being I get tired, I'd say no, because there is an inner deep conviction of the tremendous power of truth and of love, of the human community and of the willingness to learn, and learn especially from the most insignificant person. And where the wisdom of that comes out, there constantly I stand astounded to say, how foolish have you been, Beyers, that you did not see this and discover this before, and then I feel so tremendously enriched that I feel, okay, let the next day come. I am ready.

Interviewer
Can I ask you, Dr Sölle, are you often tired?

Sölle
Sure I am tired, I'm tired of saying the same thing, doing the same thing again and again. But in an inner sense, I'm not at all tired, I can't become tired with the gospel, that's a sort of self-contradiction. If the gospel is the gospel it nourishes me, and strengthens me, and I do believe that my greatest strength comes from the poor. Liberation theology has a principle, the poor are the teachers, so the teaching does not happen in Rome or Wittenberg or Amsterdam. It happens somewhere else. And today it happens where the poor are, and listening to the poor gives you an enormous strength. I was reading through the book of your country fellow-sister, Winnie Mandela, a marvellous book, where she talks about all this discrimination and hassle, from day to day, with the most cruel laws and law-like regulations of daily life for anyone there. And yet in that book I don't find even the slightest bit of

despair, frustration, tiredness, all of these moods we all have, or powerlessness. Instead of that I find in that book, in every line, strength, clarity, power, and a deep sense that truth will make us free. They have a different relation to truth than we do.

Beyers Naudé
Very true.

Sölle
I was moved when I saw that you were working on a paper with the name *Pro Veritate* (For Truth) and I think we need that more than anything else, in a world where children are growing up, watching six to eight hours' television which tells them about cat food or the new style of hairdressing or whatever — the most ridiculous things in which people are brain-washed through the unconscious messages of our culture, which are so devastating. I think that we need nothing more than truth, and in this sense I do believe that the greatest role of the church today is to be *mater et magistra*, to be a teacher. The church has to teach.

Interviewer
A mother as well as a teacher?

Sölle
A mother as well as a teacher, yes.

Beyers Naudé
I can only speak from the experience of our own country and of our own community, that this is something else which I discovered, that truth normally only is revealed to us in situations of crisis, where you are forced into the crucible, where you have to

make a choice, where you've got to get clarity in your
own mind, as to where does justice lie, where does
liberation lie, where it is no longer possible to say: I remain
neutral. There is no neutrality possible, or no true
neutrality, in a situation of crisis, and I think one of the
major problems of the church is that it was in a certain
sense educated to see itself to be a neutral body. We have
also misunderstood the concept of reconciliation so that
the church, or many parts of the church leadership,
believe that you can only truly be a reconciling agent if
you remain neutral, and that's not possible.

Sölle
No, that's not possible.

Beyers Naudé
You must first of all take your stand on the side of truth.
And then you can become a truly reconciling factor,
because then you help your opponent to discover the fact of
him or her not understanding the truth, and the moment
both these parties come to discover where truth lies, also
the truth of God's love, the truth of true commitment and
community, the truth of people living together without
fear, the moment that is discovered, then your true
reconciliation becomes a motivating and a renewing force.

Sölle
I'd like to give an example of that. On 8 May, the day
of capitulation, or of liberation, I was in Berlin
speaking to a crowd, together with the Rev. Jesse
Jackson from the United States. And he gave a very
moving speech against such neutrality, and he made
it very clear to us when he said, who talks against the
Third Reich has to talk against the Fourth Reich as
well, and with the Fourth Reich he meant South Africa.
It was a speech of power and clarity,

encouraging the people to fight against these forms of injustice, and learn anew what love and justice is.

Beyers Naudé
May I just say that I think in this respect what is happening in our country is, in a certain sense, a real acid test which the whole church in South Africa is undergoing. My feeling is that we are being tested there as never before. And I'm not only talking again about the three white Dutch Reformed Churches still supporting apartheid, I'm talking about the churches claiming to reject apartheid, claiming to seek a new community, but yet in so many respects, you know, not still being prepared to pay the price. And I think in this respect what is happening there in South Africa could possibly be to a certain degree a guidance, or

hopefully an inspiration, to other parts of the world.

Because if we are able to discover again the true meaning of what it means to be the church, to be Christian, to live in true communion and in fellowship and understanding and love and forgiveness, to build a society which is more just, to discover also the true roots of peace, it may be that in the crucible of that society, which in a certain sense is a microcosm of the whole world, of people of different cultures and languages and faiths and religions and classes being together, we may be able to set an example and mediate hope. Even if it's only a small part of the community, black and brown and white, if I may be allowed to use these racial terms, which I don't like but I have to because of our situation.

Interviewer
We are all coloured…!

Beyers Naudé
Yes, fortunately. If we are able, even a little, to discover it and begin to live it out, to enact it more meaningfully, I just hope and pray that out of that some message of encouragement and of enlightenment and of hope will come to other communities.

Sölle
Yes, and to the power elites of the first world as well. I do believe that God works through the poor and with the poor, and they are those who bring liberation forward. But they, in our historical situation, need the cooperation of Christians among these minorities. They need the support of the minorities inside, right inside of the belly of the beast. Those of my brothers and sisters, for example, in the United States, who go to the borderline of Nicaragua and tell the invading Contras and their money-givers: "Please kill us first

before you go and kill all the Nicaraguans. We are American citizens. Here's our passport." That is a wonderful witness for peace, in my eyes, and I think there are more of these than we usually know.

Beyers Naudé
And it is the same in South Africa. There are two major treason trials, which are at the present moment being forced upon the community, the one starting on 11 July, the other one later in the year: 16 people in the one case, major leaders of the society of South Africa, struggling for justice and for peace; 22 others, amongst them you have some of the most deeply committed Christians that I have ever met in my life. And I ask myself, where is this leading us to? What is going to be the response on the part of the Christian community both inside and outside South Africa? I am not saying that there could not possibly be a proof which could be forthcoming in these trials that one or more of them may have considered contemplating or supporting an act of violence.

But even if that is the case, my question is, to what degree are we in South Africa trying to listen and to understand and to discover the real message that these people are trying to convey, both to South Africa and to the world outside? Even if all of them are going to be convicted, even if all the 38 are going to be sent to prison, for prison sentences ranging from possibly 5 years to 15 or 20 years, I am convinced that the indomitable spirit of those people will not one whit be dampened or in any way subdued. They will come out of that period of imprisonment with a deeper conviction, with an inner strength, and with no hatred.

That is something which the black community in South Africa taught me. Young people going in, being tortured, being mishandled, and coming out, and I ask them, but don't you hate us whites for what you have experienced in pain and suffering? And then the answer comes, in the beginning I feared, and then I hated, and then I discovered, no, I am the one who is strong, because I have to pity this person. He is a victim, he is imprisoned in his own tragic concept, and therefore he is unfree and I am free. And, you know, once you hear that from a person who has been severely tortured, and you catch something of the tremendous warmth of that spirit of love and of community and of forgiveness, then you begin to understand that there is a totally new perspective to the Christian faith which these people in certain situations of crisis convey to you.

Interviewer
And that is why the poor are the teachers?

Sölle
Yes, that is why no one could teach us that except those who have gone through all of this, and really can tell us something about what it means to love our enemies. I mean, to love one's enemies may be the hardest thing in Christianity, in Christian faith. When I was young, coming out of a bourgeois education, I always thought: I don't have any enemies. What a strange concept! I really believed I didn't have enemies, and this was my solution to the problem of having enemies. I have no enemies. That was very typical for a young girl coming out of that culture, and it took me quite a while to understand that this is not what Jesus meant. He didn't give us this little bourgeois illusion. There are enemies, there are enemies of the human race today, who plan several terrible things for the human race. It's ridiculous to close one's eyes. To love the enemy doesn't mean to have illusions in a sort of nice, optimistic way, but it means to trust

even that enemy who is imprisoned in his tanks and atomic weapons and star wars concept, and so on and so on, that even there is that love of God hidden in this person, that person can be freed, can be liberated. I think it is a much deeper faith not to deny the reality of hostility and hate which are indeed realities, but to overcome them and to think about how people can change.

Beyers Naudé
But I would like to ask this question, Dorothee. Do you see the possibility that out of all this tension, and the agony, and the conflict, and the animosity, and the fear of so many communities around the world, do you see the possibility that out of this, let me call it, a

confessing community, a confessing movement, could emerge? Do you think such a community could be born, where people — well, first of all those who proclaim Christ and confess Christ — that on the basis of their experience and their understanding, they either intuitively or perhaps consciously begin to live and discover a deeper sense of living, of loving, of sharing, of understanding, of forgiving, of being willing also to stand up for their convictions, and if necessary suffer and die? And out of that, perhaps throughout the whole world, could such a confessing movement come forward?

I am wondering, for instance, of what happened with regard to the peace efforts here and in West Germany and in other countries. Where did these come from? I mean, all of a sudden there are thousands, in fact there are millions of people. Something had happened to them inside, and they were drawn together by a deep conviction. Now, my question is, is it impossible to hope and to expect that something similar could happen, with regard not only to the whole issue of peace, but also of justice, of the removal of fear? Is it impossible for people to come to the point of saying, well, our value systems, economic and social and cultural, these have been so distorted in many respects that we feel this is not the way in which God intended life on earth to be? That was the message which I felt very strongly at the Kirchentag, you know, in the key theme "The earth is the Lord's and the fullness thereof", and there was a totally new vision which I believe some of the young people not only received, but which they brought home to us in their understanding of what this means. And naturally their interpretation is vastly different from the theological interpretation which you will get if you walk into the study of theologians and you pull out one theological dissertation after the other — vastly

different, but isn't it more meaningful, isn't it more
existential, isn't it closer to reality?

Sölle
Yes, I couldn't agree more. Any true theological
sentence includes a condemnation, or a negative side,
so "the earth is the Lord's" means the earth is not
General Motors, not the United Food Companies, or
whoever you could mention of those who own the
earth, and you have to name the owners of the earth.
It is not the Pentagon's, even if they take most of our
woods and places to relax and make them into their
country, taking our soil from us. But I think, when
you asked me, wouldn't it be possible, I really would
say, you see as I do the signs of the times, and it
happens already before our eyes that the blind begin
to see. In my country, the peace movement grows
slowly but step by step, deep into the conservative
sector of society. The blind begin to see. It shows that
people understand what the real issue is, how peace and
justice are inter-related, and that you cannot build
peace upon militarism, but have to build it upon
justice. There is no other way to build peace. And
this happens, I think, in many many places all over
the world. Helder Camara has called them Abrahamic
minorities and this is the *Gestalt* of it right now, but I
think it grows and becomes more visible, and also the
coalitions with other people coming from different
traditions, maybe not the Christian faith but other
humanistic or religious traditions.

I have a strong sense that the respect for us
Christians working in the movement has grown so
much in the last few years. Not for the church as
such, but for those who tried to live out these new
forms of community and risk and search for truth, and
struggle for justice and peace.

Interviewer
Will there be a new Confessing Church?

Sölle
I think, in a way, what we have in liberation theology,
which is not just a new theology but a new movement
out of which a new form of theology comes, we do
already have a change in the structural church or the
dominant church. This happens through a certain
polarization which takes place, it is said often,
because we lose friends and brothers and sisters, but I
think it happens and it grows. I think some of the
World Council of Churches' proclamations already
have the quality of such confession. If you say truly it
is a sin against the Creator, the Redeemer and the
Spirit to build and test nuclear weapons, that is a
very very clear statement of faith, and not just a
statement of reason.

And if you say you cannot feed the poor with bombs,
you need something else for them, it is a similar
statement which is very clear. And I think that happens
more and more. I am thinking about the community of
scientists and engineers, which is an important group
of people, who need that conversion out of their
purposeless and meaningless doing of research for I
don't know what. But it is blind, it is highly irrational.
I think that changes already, if you recall the MIT
Conference in 1979, where they all confessed that they
did not know where to go from here, a very interesting
sign of the times, and I think that we are moving into
that direction of a confessing church which is a church
of resistance. That is the first thing to do. Maybe the
Confessing Church even was not clear enough, the
historical form of the Confessing Church in Germany,
about what resistance really meant. Most people when
they hear about the confessing church think about

Bonhoeffer. That is OK. If they think about all the
rest of them it is not OK.

Interviewer
At least half of our clergy in prison, to be harassed by
governments ... no money from the government any
more, that kind of thing?

Sölle
It means very real things about prison, as a decent
place for a person who lives in a state of injustice, as
Thoreau said.

Interviewer
Have you ever been imprisoned, as Beyers Naudé
has been banned for seven years?

Sölle
No, I haven't. I went to several things, and I am proud
of being a member of my faculty at the Union
Theological Seminary where 18 of my colleagues have
recently been for brief periods imprisoned on behalf of
South Africa.

Beyers Naudé
I am aware of that.

Sölle
For me it is a beautiful sign because some of those
colleagues, to speak frankly, are very reluctant to do
such things and go on the streets, they'd rather sit in
the library and write footnotes. But the Spirit now is
so strong, that she carries those people with them.
They just cannot stand by and stay neutral. It is
impossible in certain situations, and people understand
that and do it.

Interviewer
I think this was the first time you had the opportunity to
ask each other very difficult questions. Now, let us suppose
that this is also the last time you see each other. It could be
true, I hope not, but it could be true. What would be the
most urgent question you would like to put?

Beyers Naudé
You mean the question that we would like to put to each
other? You start, Dorothee.

Sölle
Why don't you start?

Beyers Naudé
Well, the question that I would like to put to you would
be this: Do you, in yourself, have the strength to endure
whatever may come to you by way of disappointment,
by way of rejection, by way of non-recognition, by way of
waiting, perhaps your whole life, without being able to
participate in the victory of the truth that you are
standing for? Do you believe that you will be able to
sustain yourself through these years up to the very end?

Sölle
I am thinking of a friend's answer to that when I was in a
state of despair, and had this sense of meaninglessness and
never reaching anything, and then he talked about the
cathedrals which were built during the Middle Ages.
Most of them were built over 200 years, some over 300
years even, and some of the workers in those cathedrals
never saw the whole building, they never went to pray
there, they never saw the glass and all the beautiful
things they gave their life for. And then this friend said to
me: "Listen, Dorothee, we who are building the

cathedral of peace, maybe we won't see it either. We will die before it is completed, and yet we are going to build it. We are going on even if we won't live in that building." I think that is true and in a way it fits with what I wanted to ask you. It is not a real television response but when you asked that, I just thought of asking you: "Give me your blessing my brother, I need it."

Beyers Naudé (taking her hands in his)
May I? Loving Father, this is a moment of deep and meaningful togetherness. I thank you that I know your blessing is upon both of us, and upon all of us who wish to seek truth and love and peace for the whole world. Give this to us. Help us to receive it and never to lose it. Amen.

Some other Risk books *

John V. Taylor – **WEEP NOT FOR ME**
Meditations on the cross and the resurrection

Zephania Kameeta – **WHY, O LORD?**
Psalms and sermons from Namibia

Emilio Castro – **SENT FREE**
Mission and unity in the perspective of the kingdom

Joan Puls, O.S.F. – **EVERY BUSH IS BURNING**
A spirituality for our times

Michael Kinnamon – **WHY IT MATTERS**
Personal reflections on the "Baptism, Eucharist and Ministry"
text

Allan Boesak – **WALKING ON THORNS**
The call to Christian obedience

W.J. Milligan – **THE NEW NOMADS**
Challenges facing Christians in western Europe

John Bluck – **BEYOND TECHNOLOGY**
Contexts for Christian communication

Cecil Rajendra – **SONGS FOR THE UNSUNG**
Poems on unpoetic issues like war, want and refugees

Lesslie Newbigin – **THE OTHER SIDE OF 1984**
Questions to the churches

Claudius – **ONCE UPON A TIME...**
Political fables

Rodney M. Booth – **THE WINDS OF GOD**
The Canadian churches face the 1980s

Betty Thompson – **A CHANCE TO CHANGE**
Women and men in the church

John Poulton – **THE FEAST OF LIFE**
A theological reflection on the theme "Jesus Christ – the Life of the World"

John J. Vincent – **STARTING ALL OVER AGAIN**
Hints of Jesus in the city

Ron O'Grady – **THIRD WORLD STOPOVER**
The tourism debate

C.S. Song – **THE TEARS OF LADY MENG**
A parable of people's political theology

THE KINGDOM ON ITS WAY
Meditations and music for mission

Ans J. van der Bent – **CHRISTIANS AND COMMUNISTS**
An ecumenical perspective

Huub Oosterhuis – **THE CHILDREN OF THE POOR MAN**
Part fairy story, part theological critique of attitudes towards violence and greed

Marianne Katoppo – **COMPASSIONATE AND FREE**
An Asian woman's theology

Albert H. van den Heuvel – **SHALOM AND COMBAT**
A personal struggle against racism

Rex Davis – **LOCUSTS AND WILD HONEY**
The charismatic renewal and the ecumenical movement

---

* Available from WCC Publications

From Wm. B. Eerdmans
Of related interest...

BONHOEFFER AND SOUTH AFRICA
Theology in Dialogue
By John W. de Gruchy

THE CHURCH STRUGGLE IN SOUTH AFRICA
By John W. de Gruchy

APARTHEID IS A HERESY
Edited by John W. de Gruchy and Charles Villa-Vicencio

CRYING IN THE WILDERNESS
By Desmond Tutu

HOPE AND SUFFERING
By Desmond Tutu

RESISTANCE AND HOPE
South African Essays in Honour of Beyers Naudé
Edited by Charles Villa-Vicencio and John W. de Gruchy

A MOMENT OF TRUTH
The Confession of the Dutch Reformed Mission Church, 1982
Edited by G.D. Cloete and D.J. Smit

WALKING ON THORNS
The Call to Christian Obedience
By Allan Boesak

CONTENDING IDEOLOGIES IN SOUTH AFRICA
Edited by James Leatt, Theo Kneifel, and Klaus Nürnberger